Advent

A Time of Preparation

VC
VCNETTLES INSPIRATIONS
AND LETTERS

HUTCHINSON
MISSIONARY
BAPTIST CHURCH

Advent

A Time of Preparation

A devotional of preparation led by
Pastor Cameron R. Thomas, M.Div.
Hutchinson Missionary Baptist Church

Contributing Authors

Sakia Dixon	Timothy Dixon
Celestine Drayden	Keron Forte
Jeanetta Green	Queen Green
Shermeka Hawthorne	Erica King
Gavin King	Debra Tucker
Lewis Webb, Jr.	Sandra Wood

Copyright - 2025

ISBN: 979-8-9913949-2-5

Printed in the United States

Table of Contents

A Journey into Advent

Advent is an annual observance, which is sometimes misunderstood as it occurs during what is considered the Christmas season. However, Advent is different. *Advent is a season of preparation and prayer – the awaiting of the Christ-Child.* Advent is a time of personal self-reflection, spiritual renewal, and prayer. While Christmas, the designated celebration of Jesus' birth, celebrates the fulfillment and celebration of the promise.

As we, Hutchinson Missionary Baptist Church Family and Friends, continue on our journey to build spiritual growth, commitment, and community, a group of our church's laypersons and ministers was assembled to create a devotional that celebrates the Advent Season. It is our desire that you read and reflect on the daily devotions individually, as a family, and also as a church family.

We are excited to 'walk alongside' - to walk together – as we explore through prayer, preaching, and reflection the realization of an Old Testament promise. It is our prayer that each person who adventures through this devotional is inspired and renewed, as we wait for the birth of our Savior, Jesus the Christ. *Amen.*

This Advent devotional had been developed using the 2025 daily Advent Readings and the New International Version (NIV) biblical translation.

Pastor's Introduction

What a joy it is to share in our very first **HMBC Advent Devotional**—a natural extension of the spiritual depth and communal warmth that have blossomed within our congregation over the past few years. Since my tenure began, we have intentionally embraced the observance of **Advent during our Sunday morning worship**, creating a rhythm of anticipation that beautifully culminates each year with our **Christmas Eve Candlelight Service**. Those moments of worship and light have inspired us to expand this practice—to move from a single evening of reflection to a sustained journey through the entire Advent season.

This devotional serves as a companion for that journey. Each day offers a Scripture reading, reflection, and prayer to guide your time with God. Whether read individually in quiet devotion or shared together with family, friends, or small groups, these writings are meant to center our hearts daily on the meaning of Christ's coming. I encourage you to take a few moments each day to pause, read, reflect, and pray—allowing the rhythm of Advent to shape your outlook and deepen your sense of gratitude and hope.

Each reflection was thoughtfully written by members of our Hutchinson family, whose words embody our collective faith and commitment to spiritual growth. Their voices remind us that Christ continues to speak through His people and that our shared testimony is itself a form of worship. Many thanks to Dr. Vernet C. Nettles for her leadership and commitment to seeing this project becoming a reality. This project would not have been possible without her dedication and commitment.

My prayer is that this devotional will nurture your spirit, strengthen our fellowship, and keep us attuned to the light of Christ shining among us. Together, may we journey through this season with renewed faith, expectancy, and joy.

With love and hope,

Cameron R. Thomas, M.Div.
Hutchinson Missionary Baptist Church

I'll Pray for You
Jeanetta Green

Scripture Readings
Psalm 122; Daniel 9:15-19; James 4:1-10

Focus Scripture
18Give ear, our God, and hear; open your eyes and see the desolation of the city that bears your Name. We do not make requests of you because we are righteous, but because of your great mercy.

Daniel 9:18 NIV

We often say the words "I'll pray for you." When someone shares that they are going through a difficult situation or embarking on a new venture or chapter in life, we say "I'll pray for you." Even when someone says or does something to us that we don't like, we say, "I'll pray for you." But do we? How often does "I'll pray for you" become a thoughtless response with no actual follow-up prayer?

While exiled, Daniel read the word of God as prophesied by Jeremiah and understood that his city and his people needed prayer (Daniel 9:1-4). The people may not have recognized their need, but Daniel recognized the need, so he prayed. Daniel didn't just utter thoughtless words. He petitioned God in earnest, fervent prayer for mercy on the people and the city, not because of who they were, but because of who God is. "...we do not make requests of you because we are righteous, but because of Your great mercy." (Daniel 9:18)

Praying for others is a privilege, an opportunity, and a responsibility. Prayer is a selfless and compassionate gift that we can always give. Pay attention to the needs and concerns of others (your church, community, city, the nation) and pray. Prayer and blessings are connected.

Prayer

Heavenly Father, thank you for being near whenever we pray. Thank you for the access we have to you in prayer. Open our eyes to see the needs and concern that are around us. Give us confidence to stand in the gap for others through prayer. In Jesus' name we pray. *Amen.*

Journal Questions
What are the needs that you see around you? Will you fervently pray to God to act to address those needs?

"What is your prayer today?

Community and Connection = Blessings on Blessings
Sakia Dixon

Scripture Readings
Psalm 122; Genesis 6:1-10; Hebrews 11:1-7

Focus Scriptures
[8]But Noah found favor in the eyes of the Lord.
Genesis 6:8 NIV

[1]I rejoiced with those who said to me, "Let us go to the house of the Lord."
Psalm 122:1 NIV

In Genesis 1, God began creation. He marveled at his work and said, "It was good." However, in true human form, mankind disappointed God. In Genesis 6:1-10, God observed evil of all sorts. With a grieving heart, He began to cultivate plans to eliminate all of creation. But Noah, being described as a just man, found favor in the eyes of God. By favor, Noah was chosen. By his connections, others were saved. Connections and community open the door for blessings upon blessings.

In Psalm 122, King David proclaims, "I was glad when they said unto me, let us go into the house of the Lord." In today's world, that simple declaration activates an excited call and response from the fearless and faithful, while uplifting the spirits of the sorrowful and downtrodden. In the temple of God, pain, hurt, and disappointment are released, and deliverance and forgiveness are received. It is in the house of the Lord, where strength is fortified by the fellowship and encouragement from one to the other.

Throughout scripture, God invites us to understand the power of being in fellowship with Him and with others. The house of the Lord is a safe place for unity and connection for everyone. It is there that we are able to unite with others who are walking the walk and talking the talk, day by day.

Prayer

Dear Lord, thank you for the ability to fellowship with You. Life is hard. The house of the Lord allows space for us to gather for renewal, rejuvenation, and revelation. Lord, please remind us that You have seen it all and You have also covered it all. The chastisements of our peace were upon you. Thank you, Oh God, for this church, this community, and this connection. In Jesus' name we pray. *Amen.*

Journal Questions

How does your relationship with God lead others to seek and trust in Him?

Why do you get excited about entering the House of the Lord?

What is your prayer today?

November 29

Endure to the End
Timothy Dixon

Scripture Readings:
Psalm 122; Genesis 6:11-22; Matthew 24:1-22

Focus Scripture
[12]Because of the increase of wickedness, the love of most will grow cold, [13]but the one who stands firm to the end will be saved.

Matthew 24:12-13 NIV

We are all waiting for the day when Jesus returns. His return has been a mystery since biblical times. In Matthew 24:1-22, Jesus told the disciples to look for signs. Several of those signs we are seeing today. Do not be troubled or unnerved, for "all of these things must come to pass, but the end is not yet."

Trials and tribulations are prevalent. It is easy to become discouraged and saddened by the current state of affairs. Rarely does the daily news highlight happy stories. Instead, murders, thefts, and injustices are often occurrences. Unfortunately, many are days of sorrow. The hearts of countless souls have turned cold with anger. While nations turn against each other and false prophets proclaim that the end is here, continue to find comfort in God's promises. He wants us to hold on until He returns!

During this holy season, seek and create joy and peace here on earth. Endure, yet still find time to laugh. Endure, yet still find time to be in healthy communion with others. Endure, yet still find time to love. "He who endures to the end shall be saved." Oh, what joy that will be to not have to endure any more. One day, we will embrace the beauty of His holiness. The best is *still* yet to come!

Prayer

Dear Lord, thank you for giving us a holy guide. The world is in disarray, but our souls are comforted in knowing that Jesus will return. The angels will rejoice, and the clouds will move Him through the sky. Oh, how great a day that will be. Until that time, Oh Lord, give us strength to endure. In Jesus' name we pray. *Amen.*

Journal Questions

What are your obstacles or troubles that cause you to be discouraged?

In what things, people or places, do you find encouragement and hope?

What is your prayer for today?

Weekly Reflection

What was the most significant spiritual moment or insight you experienced this week?

What challenges or obstacles did you encounter, and how did you overcome them?

What specific prayers have you seen answered or progress during this week?

What scripture, word, or message stood out to you and why?

In what ways can you continue to grow spiritually as you move into this next week of Advent?

Hope

Advent begins with a message of hope. In the first weeks of the season, we focus, with anticipation, on Christ's second coming while, at the same time, reflecting on his first coming in Bethlehem. Hope is the trust that God will fulfill His promises, just as He did with the coming of the Messiah.

Scripture Readings
Isaiah 2:1-5; Psalm 122; Romans 13:11-14; Matthew 24:36-44

Sermon Notes

December 1

Embracing a Pathway to a Peaceful Life
Celestine Drayden

Scripture Readings
Psalm 124; Genesis 8:1-19; Romans 6:1-11

Focus Scripture
⁴We were therefore buried with him through baptism into death in order that, just as Christ was raised from the dead through the glory of the Father, we too may live a new life.

Romans 6:4 NIV

The journey to a peaceful life begins with the recognition that, through Christ, believers are called to leave behind their old way of living and embrace a new existence grounded in God's grace. This transformed life is not about striving to earn salvation but about living in a way that reflects God's love and righteousness. As Paul teaches in Romans, baptism signifies being buried with Christ and raised to new life, inviting us to walk in freedom from sin's power.

Living out this new identity means dedicating ourselves to God's ways, seeking to bear fruit such as good works, obedience, peace, and a deeper relationship with God. We are empowered by the Holy Spirit to resist temptation, pursue righteousness, and let our lives serve as a testimony to the redeeming power of God at work within us. By following this path, we experience not only personal transformation but also the peace that comes from aligning our lives with God's purpose.

Prayer

Gracious God, thank you for the gift of new life through Jesus Christ. Help us remember that we are dead to sin and alive to You. Grant us the strength to resist temptation and the courage to walk the path of righteousness. Fill our hearts with Your Spirit so that our lives may bear fruit worthy of our calling. Guide us each day to reflect your love, mercy, peace, and truth in all we do. In Jesus' name we pray. **Amen.**

Journal Questions
What is your prayer today?

December 2

When Promises Seem Delayed
Lewis Webb, Jr.

Scripture Readings
Psalm 124; Genesis 9:1-17; Hebrews 11:32-40

Focus Scripture

[32]*And what more shall I say? I do not have time to tell about Gideon, Barak, Samson and Jephthah, about David and Samuel and the prophets,*[33]*who through faith conquered kingdoms, administered justice, and gained what was promised; who shut the mouths of lions,*[34]*quenched the fury of the flames, and escaped the edge of the sword; whose weakness was turned to strength; and who became powerful in battle and routed foreign armies.*

Hebrews 11:32-34 NIV

When we think of faith, we often picture answered prayers, miracles, and blessings. But Hebrews 11 reminds us that faith is much deeper than quick victories or easy wins. The heroes listed—Gideon, Samson, David, Samuel, and so many others— faced battles, fears, persecution, and even death. Yet, they pressed forward because they believed in a God who was greater than their circumstances.

Some saw miraculous outcomes—kingdoms conquered, lions' mouths shut, and flames extinguished. Others endured unimaginable trials—mockery, imprisonment, and even death. Still, they remained faithful, knowing God had prepared "something better."

11

This passage speaks to us today. Sometimes we feel like we're doing everything right—praying, serving, believing—and yet the breakthrough doesn't come as quickly as we hoped. In those moments, Hebrews 11 reminds us that faith isn't about immediate results, it's about trusting God's eternal plan. Their story becomes our encouragement: you are not alone in the struggle, and your faith has eternal impact.

Prayer

Heavenly Father, thank You for the examples of faith-filled believers who endured so much and still trusted You. Teach me to walk with that same courage. When I feel weak, remind me that You are my strength. May my life reflect a faith that endures and points others to Your greater promise. In Jesus' name we pray. *Amen.*

Journal Questions:
How do you trust God even when the outcome doesn't look like what you expected?

What is your prayer today?

Peace in The Time of Despair
Keron Forte

Scripture Readings
Psalm 124; Isaiah 54:1-10; Matthew 24:23-35

Focus Scripture
[10]"*Though the mountains be shaken and the hills be removed, yet my unfailing love for you will not be shaken nor my covenant of peace be removed," says the Lord, who has compassion on you.*

Isaiah 54:10 NIV

We have all experienced times when things did not go the way we wanted them to. It may have been a job offer we thought we had. A promotion that passed us by. A marriage we thought would take place. A child we longed to have. Whatever the situation may be, it has caused us to be in despair. It is in these times that Jesus says He has compassion on us (Isaiah 54:8). The job offer or promotion that passed us by because God has something better in store for us. The marriage has not taken place because God knows the timing is not right. The child you long to give birth to has not happened because God knows there are children in the world that need to be adopted and loved.

The Lord is always on our side. He gives us peace in the time of despair. "Praise be to the Lord...the Maker of heaven and earth" (Psalm 124: 6, 8). Our hope is in His name.

Prayer

Dear Lord, give us peace in our time of despair. You know what is best for us. Help us to know that your unfailing love will see us through. In Jesus' name we pray. **Amen.**

Journal Questions

What challenges are you experiencing today that are causing you despair?

In what areas of your life are you experiencing the peace of God?

What is your prayer today?

December 4

Peaceful Decisions with Divine Guidance
Celestine Drayden

Scripture Readings
Psalm 72:1-7; 18-19; Isaiah 4:2-6; Acts 1:12-17,21-26

Focus Scripture
26Then they cast lots, and the lot fell to Matthias; so he was added to the eleven apostles.

Acts 1:26 NIV

Have you ever experienced situations where the choices before you were unclear? Life often presents us with numerous options. In today's devotion, we reflect on a pivotal moment in the apostles' lives that occurred after the betrayal and death of Judas Iscariot. The apostles faced a significant decision: who would replace Judas to continue carrying out God's word and spreading the gospel in Jerusalem and throughout the earth? The remaining apostles, along with other believers, prayed for God's guidance in selecting a new apostle (Acts 1:21-22). They presented two candidates: Joseph called Barsabbas (also known as Justus) and Matthias (Acts 1:23). Through prayer and the casting of lots, Matthias was chosen, demonstrating divine guidance and the importance of collective discernment (Acts 1:24-26).

Today's passage emphasizes unity, prayer, and reliance on God's wisdom during times of uncertainty. The apostles prayed collectively, illustrating that spiritual decisions should involve the community. The qualifications for apostleship—being a witness

15

from John's baptism to Jesus' ascension—highlight the importance of personal experience.

Casting lots reminds us that God ultimately decides, even when human perspectives differ; henceforth, we should remain receptive to unexpected opportunities and new beginnings chosen by God. We are encouraged to make our life-choices personal or communal—through prayerful discernment and peace. Like Matthias, our faithfulness prepares us for unforeseen peaceful opportunities.

Prayer

Dear Lord God, in times of transition, help us seek your guidance with humble hearts. May we trust your direction and accept your choices. Unite us as a community of believers, centered on Christ and open to your Spirit's movement. In Jesus' name we pray. *Amen.*

Journal Questions
What choices do you have to make today?

What is your prayer today?

Faith That Brings the Rain
Lewis Webb, Jr.

Scripture Readings
Psalm 72:1-7; 18-19; Isaiah 30:19-26; Acts 13:16-25

Focus Scripture
[23]*He will also send you rain for the seed you sow in the ground, and the food that comes from the land will be rich and plentiful. In that day your cattle will graze in broad meadows.*
Isaiah 30:23 NIV

Faith is not only believing that God can bless—it's trusting that He will, in His time and in His way. Isaiah paints a picture of abundance after a season of drought. The rain doesn't just fall randomly—it comes after the seed is sown. God promises to send increase when we've planted in faith.

There are moments when it feels like our prayers, service, or sacrifices are hidden beneath dry soil. But God is faithful. When we keep sowing in faith—our time, our worship, our love. He sends the rain that transforms what we've planted into something rich and plentiful.

This passage reminds us that faith is both action and expectation. We sow, even when the ground looks barren. We trust, even when the skies look empty. And In due season, God sends the rain of provision, renewal, and reward.

So, keep sowing. Keep believing. The same God who gives the seed will send the rain.

Prayer

Lord, thank You for being the God of both the seed and the harvest. Strengthen my faith to keep sowing even when I cannot yet see the rain. Remind me that You are faithful to provide, restore, and bless in Your perfect timing. Let my life yield fruit that brings glory to Your name. In Jesus' name we pray. *Amen.*

Journal Questions

What seeds are you planting in faith right now that you need to trust God to water?

What small signs of rain have you witnessed that prompts you to express your gratitude to God?

What is your prayer today?

Who Are You?
Keron Forte

Scripture Readings:
Psalm 72:1-7; 18-19; Isaiah 40:1-11; John 1:19-28

Focus Scripture
[22]Finally they said, "Who are you? Give us an answer to take back to those who sent us. What do you say about yourself?"
John 1:22 NIV

Have you ever wondered who somebody was, especially if they were acting in a manner that was unusual or out of the ordinary? Or you may see someone who looks familiar and wonder who that person is? It is common to ask this question when you see someone you are not sure about. That is what is happening in the scripture for today. The Jewish leaders questioned all of the things John the Baptist was doing as he was preparing the way for the Lord. They asked him if he was the Messiah. Was he Elijah? Was he a prophet? John's answer was, "No" (John 1:21). "Who Are You?" the Pharisees asked (John 1:22). He replied in the words of Isaiah the prophet, "I am the voice of one calling in the wilderness, 'Make straight the way for the Lord'" (John 1:23). Isaiah emphasized, "And the glory of the Lord will be revealed (Isaiah 40:5). Who do you say the Lord is? Who is He to you?

Prayer
Dear Lord, give me the tenacity to speak boldly about Your Son whenever someone asks me who He is. He is the Messiah. The

Chosen One. Let me be His voice today. In Jesus' name we pray. *Amen.*

Journal Questions
The next time someone asks you who the Lord is, what will you tell them?

What is one way you can tell someone about Jesus, tomorrow?

What is your prayer today?

Weekly Reflection

What was the most significant spiritual moment or insight you experienced this week?

What challenges or obstacles did you encounter, and how did you overcome them?

What specific prayers have you seen answered or progress during this week?

What scripture, word, or message stood out to you and why?

In what ways can you continue to grow spiritually as you move into this next week of Advent?

Second Sunday of Advent
December 7

Peace

The second virtue of Advent is peace. Peace is a gift that Christ brought to the world when He was born in the stable. The birth, life, and promise of the Christ Child would bring peace to the nations and reconciliation with God, personal peace, and peace within the community of nations.

Scripture Readings
Isaiah 11:1-10; Psalm 72:1-7, 18-19; Romans 15:4-13; Matthew 3:1-12

Sermon Notes

Living a Peaceful Life with Christ
Debra Tucker

Scripture Readings
Psalm 21; Isaiah 24:1-16a; 1 Thessalonians 4:1-12

Focus Scripture
[11]and to make it your ambition to lead a quiet life: You should mind your own business and work with your hands, just as we told you,
I Thessalonians 4:11 NIV

Life can have you like a rubber band. It is either at ease or being stretched. And if it's stretched too tightly, it can break. Believe me, I have reached that breaking point many times in life. You are not at peace, and do not feel the joy that comes from a relationship with God because you are stretched, tense, and not at ease. It seems as if all the teaching, studying, and life experiences have slipped through the cracks. You are trying to do things with your limited powers and ignore the fact that God is *all* powerful and He is in control. Snap back, please.

The way to find the peaceful life of a rubber band at ease is to surrender and rest in the Lord. Our surrendered heart finds peace in the Lord and that attitude carries over into peaceful relationships with others. If you find peace in Him, you are not stretched. Paul reminds the Thessalonians in this chapter, to continue to please God in their lives by avoiding their many sins, loving one another, and living as good citizens in a secular world. These words still speak to our lives today. Read it! It's in the

Bible. It reminds us that peace of mind comes when we stand on the many promises of God.

Trust me. As we stand on His promises and get close to Him, His image is stamped on us. Surrender to Him. To do His work, you are at ease. If you are busy praying and praising Him, you're at peace because you are where He wants you to be, doing what He created you to do. Many of us long for that quiet life, trying to mind our own business and work hard with our own hands, but the chaos of the world steals our peace. No God. No Peace.

Let the Holy Spirit, through faith and prayer lead your direction, take over your life, and run it. Be still, get quiet, mind your business, work hard, and trust Him. This is living a peaceful life with Christ.

Prayer

Father God, we thank you today for being the judge in our lives, deciding our outlook no matter the circumstances. Help us to find peace with You when our rubber band of life is stretched and ready to break. May we find Peace in Christ that flows from one heart to the next. In Jesus' name we pray. *Amen*

Journal Questions

What is your prayer today?

December 9

Victory Belongs to Jesus
Shermeka Hawthorne

Scripture Readings
Psalm 21; Isaiah 41:14-20; Romans 15:14-21

Focus Scripture
[15]See, I will make you into a threshing sledge, new and sharp, with many teeth. You will thresh the mountains and crush them, and reduce the hills to chaff. [16]You will winnow them, the wind will pick them up, and a gale will blow them away. But you will rejoice in the Lord and glory in the Holy One of Israel.

Isaiah 41:15-16 NIV

I am certain it is almost impossible to know the number of people who want to experience victory. I dare say that everyone likely wants to experience the joy and accomplishment that comes with winning. In fact, being victorious is considered a fundamental human desire.

In Isaiah 41, we see the Prophet Isaiah speaking to the people of Israel during their Babylonian exile. In this chapter, Isaiah is giving a message of hope and reassurance to those in captivity. This message is a reminder of God's supreme power and presence that aides us in overcoming various challenges we face. The metaphor of the threshing sledge is used to show how strong we can become only when we allow God to work in us. By inviting God to reign in our lives, we are blessed to experience victory over all obstacles that come our way.

Todd Dulaney has a song entitled "Victory Belongs to Jesus." I encourage you to listen to that song today to be reminded that if we want to experience true victory, we must invest our time in Him. As disciples of Christ, we are tasked with saving lost souls. We are most definitely victorious in this by the aide of Jesus Christ.

Prayer

Gracious God, our Father. We thank you for victories won and those yet to come. Help us to always follow you and your ways so that we can experience victory not only in our personal lives, but also in winning souls for you. Help us to remember that with you as our Lord and King, no one can overcome us. In Jesus' name we pray. **Amen.**

Journal Questions
What is your prayer today?

Promise
Queen Green

Scripture Readings
Psalm 21; Genesis 15:1-18; Matthew 12:33-37

Focus Scriptures
²You have granted him his heart's desire and have not withheld the request of his lips.

Psalm 21:2 NIV

⁴Then the word of the Lord came to him: "This man will not be your heir, but a son who is your own flesh and blood will be your heir.

Genesis 15:4 NIV

³³Make a tree good and its fruit will be good...

Matthew 12:33a NIV

A promise can bring a feeling of hope and joy, depending on what the promise is. It can also cause one to rejoice and praise. Growing up in the "Baby Boomer" generation, this season has always been a season of joy and anticipation because requests and promises were made. We looked for the good from the good. The desires of our hearts were made, and we believed the promises were going to be kept. The wait felt like forever. Father, You are the reward.

My mind reflects as we make preparation to celebrate the birth of the Messiah, the long-awaited promise, the one who gave up His Glory to come and dwell among men. Those who heard and believed waited many years for the promise to be fulfilled. They waited attentively with joy in their hearts for this precious promise.

As our hearts mature in Christ, we understand the true meaning for the season. We are so very thankful that the ultimate Promise Keeper fulfilled His word. We celebrate the birth of our Wonderful Counselor - the one King David loved, trusted, and never withheld his desires, and they were many. He was the source of David's strength and the solid foundation of his joy. Jesus is that solid Rock for us today. He is our hope and the joy of our salvation. On this day, let us rejoice and praise His Holy name forever and ever.

Prayer

Our Heavenly Father, we thank you for sending us your Son, the one the world waited so long for his arrival, down through forty-two generations. Our Dear Father, as we celebrate the birth of Jesus Christ, may our hearts be filled with great joy and hope, today and forevermore. Thank you for keeping your promise. In Jesus' name we pray. *Amen*

Journal Questions
What is your prayer today?

December 11

True Faithfulness and Loyalty
Debra Tucker

Scripture Readings
Psalm 146:5-10; Ruth 1:6-18; 2 Peter 3:1-10

Focus Scripture
[16]But Ruth replied, "Don't urge me to leave you or to turn back from you. Where you go I will go, and where you stay I will stay. Your people will be my people and your God my God.

Ruth 1:16 NIV

I am deeply moved by Ruth's story that exemplifies faithfulness and loyalty to Naomi, her mother-in-law. This story of love between Ruth and Naomi, caught in the middle of the bloody battles of Judges and the wars of 1 Samuel, teaches a valuable lesson that has raised the eyebrows of many readers. The entire Book of Ruth gives great encouragement as God provides an example of godly behavior in the midst of widespread ungodliness. Out of a shared, common grief, the bond was real between Ruth and Naomi. Although Naomi offered Ruth freedom from the responsibility of remaining and taking care of her, Ruth committed herself to stay. Despite different races, cultures, or backgrounds, a pure, selfless bond of love united these two women who had so little in common. Facing challenges with poverty, being an alien in a foreign land, and being alone, Ruth stayed focused on her present, not her past situations with undying faithfulness and loyalty.

It is evident that Naomi played a crucial role in shaping Ruth's faith by serving as a mentor, guide, and example of steadfast faith. Ruth embraces loyalty and faithfulness to God and adapts to a new life of peace, joy, and love. There is hope even during the most devastating times of your life. Thanks be to God for using unlikely people for His purpose when life seems hopeless.

Prayer

Gracious Father, whose lovingkindness never fails, thank you for your unchanging loyalty. In response, may we all seek to be loyal to you and to one another, regardless of the ups and downs in life we may face. In Jesus' name we pray. *Amen.*

Journal Questions
What is your prayer today?

Stay Ready, So You Don't Have To Get Ready
Shermeka Hawthorne

Scripture Readings
Psalm 146:5-10; Ruth 4:13-17; 2 Peter 3:11-18

Focus Scriptures

[17]Therefore, dear friends, since you have been forewarned, be on your guard so that you may not be carried away by the error of the lawless and fall from your secure position. [18]But grow in the grace and knowledge of our Lord and Savior Jesus Christ. To him be glory both now and forever! Amen.

2 Peter 3:17-18 NIV

In the immediate days leading up to and on Tuesday, September 23, 2025, my Instagram timeline was filled with talk of the rapture that was predicted to take place that day. A humorous reel/video clip asked for sightings of certain famous gospel artists well known for their love of Christ, to confirm if the rapture had actually taken place. While I fully believed this particular social media influencer was not really thinking the rapture was upon us, I did wonder how many people were indeed anxious or even scared at the thought of Jesus' second coming and what it means as it relates to their salvation.

In this text, Apostle Peter is writing to believers, advising them and us to live godly lives as we look forward to "a new heaven and a new earth." This passage ends with Peter directing us to "grow in the grace and knowledge of our Lord and Savior" (II Peter 3:18). Having the knowledge of who Christ is should compel us to walk in the ways He would have us walk and live in a way that embodies Him. Knowing Christ also gives us the assurance that His grace is sufficient and offers us salvation. With this, we should be confident that though we do not know exactly when God is coming back, we definitely will be ready for His return.

Prayer

Gracious God, our Father, we thank you for your patience. Grant us the wisdom to live in a way that is pleasing unto you. Give us direction as we walk this journey of faith so that we can have assurance that whenever you decide to come back, we will be going with you. In Jesus' name we pray. *Amen.*

Journal Questions
What is your prayer today?

A Change is Going to Come
Queen Green

Scripture Readings
Psalm 146:5-10; 1 Samuel 2:1-8; Luke 3:1-18

Focus Scriptures

[1] Then Hannah prayed and said: "My heart rejoices in the Lord; In the Lord my horn is lifted high. My mouth boasts over my enemies, for I delight in your deliverance."

1 Samuel 2:1 NIV

[4] As it is written in the book of Isaiah the prophet: "A voice of one is calling in the wildness, 'Prepare the way for the Lord, make straight paths for Him.'

Luke 3:4 NIV

At a time of political unrest, in the midst of the Civil Rights Movement, Sam Cooke's wrote and sang "A Change is Gonna Come." His song told of years of hardship and frustration, but the promise that things would change. Cooke's hope was to live in a world where equality for all would exist.

In this season of prayer and spiritual renewal, our minds reflect on another type of political unrest. John, fulfilling the prophesy of Isaiah, calling out in the wilderness, declared that a change is going to come. "Prepare the way of the Lord, make His path straight..." for all mankind is going to see the salvation of the Lord. In other words, let everyone rejoice, make ready for spiritual disruption - the King is on his way.

In this season we reflect on the waiting, hope, and anticipation of the Messiah. We can also feel the heart of Hannah being barren praying to God for a son. Hannah cried out that a change is going to come. Hannah loved and trusted God, she prayed for a child, not to keep for herself, but to give back to God. God gave her a deliverance of victory.

Therefore, Hannah rejoiced in the Lord, because she found strength in Him, and her dignity was restored. Today, let us have that Hannah spirit. Let our hearts rejoice in the Lord, with love, hope, and peace for a time like this. There is no one like our Heavenly Father. He is worthy to be praised.

Prayer

Our Dear Heavenly Father, we celebrate You. Father, we cry out as Hannah did, thanking You for keeping us. Our hearts rejoice in you, Lord. There is no one like You. You are the author of victory, the giver of strength, and the deliverer of our hope. We thank you for this Advent season and every blessing that You shower down on us. Father, in Jesus' we pray. **Amen.**

Journal Questions
What is your prayer today?

Weekly Reflection

What was the most significant spiritual moment or insight you experienced this week?

What challenges or obstacles did you encounter, and how did you overcome them?

What specific prayers have you seen answered or progress during this week?

What scripture, word, or message stood out to you and why?

In what ways can you continue to grow spiritually as you move into this next week of Advent?

The season pivots toward the virtue of joy. Gaudete! Waiting for Christ's coming is not sorrowful! The birth of Christ brings us the joy of salvation. Joy is grounded in the realization that God is with us. Pope Francis reminds us that "the joy of the Gospel fills the hearts and lives of all who encounter Jesus."

We need to foster joy in our lives, a joy that recognizes God is near. Joy does not ignore the hardships of life, it sees beyond them because we know that Christ has entered the world.

Scripture Readings
Isaiah 35:1-10; Psalm 146:5-10 or *Luke 1:46b-55*;
James 5:7-10; Matthew 11:2-11

Sermon Notes

Time for Healing
Sandra Wood

Scripture Readings
Psalm 42; Isaiah 29:17-24; Acts 5:12-16

Focus Scripture
[14]*Nevertheless, more and more men and women believed in the Lord and were added to their number.*

Acts 5:14 NIV

In this season, we celebrate and commemorate the days leading up to the birth of Christ. This is a joyous time of family and fellowship. We see happiness all around us.

The Apostles performed many miracles in this chapter of Acts. Because of this, believers came from near and far to receive blessings and healing. Some believed that passing through Peter's shadow would heal them.

According to the scripture, all who came were healed. We know that even in this joyous season, there are those that are sick and in need of healing. The holidays, while joyous to many, can bring great sadness to others. This could be due to an unresolved conflict within our family. It could be that we are facing other issues alone. No matter the problem, we should do as those did in this scripture. Whether it is physical, mental, emotional, spiritual, or even financial healing that is needed, I want you to know that healing is possible. The common denominator for the people in this scripture was "faith." They all believed they would be healed, and they were.

In this season, whatever you are in need of, have faith and believe God for your healing.

Prayer

Dear Heavenly Father, we come to you with humble hearts. Lord, we know that we are not perfect, but you are. Forgive us our sins and give us a clean heart. Dear Father, we ask that you heal whatever is wrong in our lives and in our bodies. We love you and want to do what is pleasing to you. We praise you in advance for our healing. In Jesus' name we pray. *Amen.*

Journal Questions
What is your prayer today?

Are you in need of healing today? Are you ready for your faith to make you whole?

December 16

A Call to Persevere
Sandra Wood

Scripture Readings
Psalm 42; Ezekiel 47:1-12; Jude 1:17-25

Focus Scripture
[24]*To him who is able to keep you from stumbling and to present you before his glorious presence without fault and with great joy—* [25] *to the only God our Savior be glory, majesty, power and authority, through Jesus Christ our Lord, before all ages, now and forevermore! Amen.*

Jude1:24-25 NIV

As in the previous day's devotional, this scripture refers to things that the apostles of Jesus Christ foretold. They said that in the last days there would be those that do not recognize God. There will be people led by their own ungodly desires. Their aim is to get what they want with no regard to the Spirit of God. The apostles of Jesus Christ predicted that it would be these ungodly, selfish, and materialistic ones that would divide us.

You have heard the saying that there is nothing new under the sun. We can look at the world today and know that what the apostles had foreseen has come to pass. We have those in high places that are seemingly being led by selfish wants and needs. There is division everywhere as a result. Division among families, governments and even churches are some examples. This has caused many to suffer and many to question where God is in all of this.

God is still in charge. We should remain steadfast in God's love and continue to pray without ceasing. We must persevere. Whenever possible, we should try to bring those who may not have their focus on God to understand that His way is the only way. Only God with all his majesty, dominion and power can keep us from falling.

Prayer

Dear Heavenly Father, we come to you humbly. We ask that you forgive our transgressions, Lord. We fall short sometimes, but we thank you for always forgiving us. In this time of division throughout the land, we ask that you keep us strong and committed to Your will and Your way. Lord, touch the hearts of those wishing to sow discord and be merciful to those who doubt you. In Jesus' name we pray. *Amen.*

Journal Questions
What steps can you take to make sure you survive in these trying times?

What can you do to become a part of the solution?

What is your prayer today?

December 17

Cast Your Cares Upon The Lord
Sandra Wood

Scripture Readings
Psalm 42; Zechariah 8:1-17; Matthew 8:14-17,28-34

Focus Scripture
⁵Why, my soul, are you downcast? Why so disturbed within me? Put your hope in God, for I will yet praise him, my Savior and my God. ⁶My soul is downcast within me; therefore I will remember you from the land of the Jordan, the heights of Hermon—from Mount Mizar.

Psalm 42:5-6 NIV

In this Psalm, the writer is remembering the joyous days of serving the Lord. Remembering and appreciating living in the shadow and wonder of God. He goes through many reflections of a time that he was covered by the goodness of God.

He also speaks of his distress, his depression, and his sorrows. There are times that he is teary eyed. Unbelievers question him as to "Where is his God" throughout his challenges. The writer makes it plain that even through tumultuous times, he will still praise his Savior and his God.

For each of us, life is full of ups and downs, tragedies and triumphs, and happiness and sadness. It is always easy to be thankful and praise God when things are going well. Today, be reminded that even when things start to look bad, God is still there.

Sometimes you may find yourself with tears in your eyes. Depression may come and it may seem like there is no way out. We should understand as the writer of this Psalm did - that through it all God is still there. He is still present, and he is orchestrating things in a way that we will never understand with our human minds. So, when things get tough, remember to still praise Him with all your heart and soul. Trust your all-knowing God.

Prayer

Dear Heavenly Father, we thank you for your love and kindness even through our imperfections. Thank you for being a forgiving God. Dear Lord, we ask that you keep us in your loving care always as we submit to your Holy will. At times, things do not go as smoothly as we would like. We are troubled sometimes. Even then, we praise you and we thank you. In Jesus' name we pray. **Amen.**

Journal Questions
Will you praise God even in times of trouble?

What is your prayer today?

The Eternal Filling Station
Erica King

Scripture Readings
Psalm 80:1-7,17-19; 2 Samuel 7:1-17; Galatians 3:23-29

Focus Scripture
7Restore us, God Almighty; make your face shine on us, that we may be saved.

Psalm 80:7 NIV

Have you ever run out of gas and been stuck? It's not a good feeling. It didn't matter that you had the newest model car off the lot or just received a tune-up; because the tank was empty, you couldn't go any further.

In Psalm 80, God's people found themselves spiritually stuck. They cannot continue without help. They cry out, "Restore us, O God; make your face shine on us, that we may be saved."

We are a lot like a car without gas; stuck and unable to go. We run dry trying to live in our own strength. Just like the vehicle stops, we are forced to surrender our control to Jesus; crying Lord, fill me, I need you!

God hears our cries. In 2 Samuel 7, God's promise to David is fulfilled through Jesus, the son of David. Jesus came to bring eternal restoration and salvation. Not only was God's people's cries answered, but He sent an eternal filling station.

At Advent, we remember that Jesus entered the world to rescue His people, to fill our empty lives with His grace, and to shine the light of God's face upon us forever.

Prayer

Lord, I confess how often I try to run on empty- relying on my own strength and forgetting that you alone can fill me. Thank you for sending Jesus to restore what was broken and to shine Your face upon me. Fill my heart with Your presence this Advent season so I may live in the fullness of Your grace and depend on You daily. In Jesus' name we pray. *Amen.*

Journal Questions

Where in your life do you feel "empty" or stuck right now?

How can you invite Jesus to fill that space with His presence and strength?

What is your prayer today?

December 19

Promise Kept
Erica King

Scripture Readings
Psalm 80:1-7, 17-19; 2 Samuel 7:18-22; Galatians 4:1-7

Focus Scripture
[18a]Then King David went in and sat before the Lord, and he said: "Who am I, Sovereign Lord, and what is my family, that you have brought me this far? [20] "What more can David say to you? For you know your servant, Sovereign Lord. [21]For the sake of your word and according to your will, you have done this great thing and made it known to your servant. [22]"How great you are, Sovereign Lord! There is no one like you, and there is no God but you, as we have heard with our own ears.

2 Samuel 7:18a, 20-22 NIV

"I promise." Those two simple words carry great weight. When someone makes a promise, we expect it to happen - we place our trust in them. But what happens when the promise seems impossible?

God promised King David that one of his sons would sit on the throne forever. David had a couple of sons and grandsons follow behind him with the royal title, but with each passing one, they all found a way to royally mess up. Their failures made the promise look fragile. Could God's word really stand through the brokenness of man?

The answer came on a silent night in Bethlehem. Jesus, descendant of David, son of God, was born into the world.

45

Conceived by the Holy Spirit, born of the Virgin Mary, fully man and fully God - He came as the promised King. His purpose was to bring the new covenant, to redeem His people, and to secure our adoption as children of God.

God's promise was kept, and His faithfulness is proven.

Prayer

Faithful God, thank You for keeping every promise. Help me to trust Your Word even when I can't see the outcome. Remind me that in Jesus, Your faithfulness is forever proven. In Jesus' name we pray. *Amen.*

Journal Questions

When have you doubted God's promises because of your circumstances?

How does remembering Jesus' birth help you trust His faithfulness today?

What is your prayer today?

December 20

From Cry to Confidence
Erica King

Scripture Readings
Psalm 80:1-7,17-19; 2 Samuel 7:23-29; John 3:31-36

Focus Scripture
[19]Restore us, Lord God Almighty; make your face shine on us, that we may be saved.

Psalm 80:19 NIV

[28]Sovereign Lord, you are God! Your covenant is trustworthy, and you have promised these good things to your servant. [29]Now be pleased to bless the house of your servant, that it may continue forever in your sight; for you, Sovereign Lord, have spoken, and with your blessing the house of your servant will be blessed forever.

2 Samuel 7:28–29 NIV

A cry, a fulfilled promise, but now what? God's people cried out, "Restore us, O God; make your face shine on us, that we may be saved." They couldn't move forward without God's help.

God answered by keeping His covenant promise to David, sending the forever king - Jesus, Son of God, and Son of David. But now what? This was just the beginning of the good news for us.

Jesus, 100% man and 100% God, lived a perfect life in this broken world. He was tempted and tried, just like you and I are, but He never gave in to the enticing things. He was then mocked, beaten on our behalf, and eventually nailed to a cross for a death sentence only we deserved. He stayed dead for three days, but then He did something no one had ever done before. He defeated death. He won! How is that so? On the third day of death, He arose and changed eternity's outcome for you and me!

This means God heard His people's cries and sent help through Jesus, the forever king. Through Jesus, God's face can now shine upon us, granting us forgiveness, life, restoration, and the gift of the Holy Spirit. The eternal death we deserve for our sin is now defeated and forgiven by God's grace through faith in Christ Jesus alone for the glory of God alone! What once was only a cry for help has become our confident hope.

Prayer

Father, thank You for turning our cry for help into hope through Your victory on the cross. Fill my heart with gratitude and confidence in Your saving grace today. In Jesus' name we pray. **Amen.**

Journal Questions
How does knowing that Jesus defeated death change the way you face challenges or moments of fear today?

What is your prayer today?

Weekly Reflection

What was the most significant spiritual moment or insight you experienced this week?

What challenges or obstacles did you encounter, and how did you overcome them?

What specific prayers have you seen answered or progress during this week?

What scripture, word, or message stood out to you and why?

In what ways can you continue to grow spiritually as you move into this next week of Advent?

The final virtue of Advent is love, the greatest of all virtues. Love is why Jesus came into the world. God loved us so much that He prepared a path for us to be restored unto him. Scripture says that love never fails; it protects, hopes, and perseveres. "And now these three remain: faith, hope, and love. But greatest of these is love." The greatest gift of Love is the birth and life of Jesus, the Christ-child, our Savior.

Scripture Readings
Isaiah 7:10-16; Psalm 80:1-7, 17-19; Romans 1:1-7;
Matthew 1:18-25

Sermon Notes

We're Waiting
Gavin King

Scripture Readings
Luke 1:46b-55; Isaiah 33:17-22; Revelation 22:6-7,18-20

Focus Scripture
[6]The angel said to me, "These words are trustworthy and true. The Lord, the God who inspires the prophets, sent his angel to show his servants the things that must soon take place." [7]"Look, I am coming soon! Blessed is the one who keeps the words of the prophecy written in this scroll." [20]He who testifies to these things says, "Yes, I am coming soon." Amen. Come, Lord Jesus.
Revelation 22:6-7,20 NIV

Advent is a season of waiting—not passive waiting, but holy anticipation. At Christmas, we remember Christ's first coming in the manger, and we look forward to His second coming in glory. Revelation 22, the final chapter of Scriptures, echoes this longing: "Come, Lord Jesus." It's the cry of every heart that has tasted grace and longs for restoration.

Jesus doesn't just promise to come—He says He is coming soon. That word stirs urgency, but also comfort. It reminds us that history is not random, and our lives are not forgotten. The Alpha and Omega has written the final word, and it is one of complete redemption.

Come what may, we have this hope: just as surely as Jesus came to us in Bethlehem, He will come again to make everything right. The broken will be healed. The weary will find rest. The waiting will be over. This Advent, let us live in that hope. Let our hearts echo the final prayer of Scripture as we wait: "Amen. Come, Lord Jesus."

Prayer

Lord Jesus, in this season of Advent, teach us to wait with faith and joy. Let your promise stir our hearts and shape our days. May we live in the light of Your coming—past, present, and future—and find peace in the truth that You are making all things new. Come, Lord Jesus. In Jesus' name we pray. *Amen.*

Journal Questions

How do I respond to the promise that Jesus is coming soon?

What areas of my life need healing and wholeness?

What does it mean to trust that history is not random, and my life is not forgotten?

What is your prayer today?

December 23

A Promise Fulfilled
Gavin King

Scripture Readings
Luke 1:46b-55; 2 Samuel 7:18, 23-29; Galatians 3:6-14

Focus Scripture
[12]The law is not based on faith; on the contrary, it says, "The person who does these things will live by them.[13]Christ redeemed us from the curse of the law by becoming a curse for us, for it is written: "Cursed is everyone who is hung on a pole." [14]He redeemed us in order that the blessing given to Abraham might come to the Gentiles through Christ Jesus, so that by faith we might receive the promise of the Spirit.

Galatians 3:12-14 NIV

Advent is a season of promise—a time to remember that God's plan of redemption began long before the manger. In Galatians 3, Paul reminds us that the blessing of salvation was never earned by law but received by faith, just as Abraham believed and was counted righteous.

This passage points us to the heart of Advent: the fulfillment of God's promise through Jesus Christ. Christ came to redeem us from the curse of the law by becoming a curse for us (Galatians 3:13), so that the blessing given to Abraham might come to all people through faith.

As we wait for Christ's return, we do so not by striving, but by trusting. Advent invites us to rest in the finished work of Jesus, who came not to burden us with rules but to free us with grace.

53

The child in the manger is the Savior on the cross—the one who brings righteousness to those who believe. This season, let us receive the gift of faith anew and rejoice in the promise fulfilled.

Prayer

Gracious God, thank You for the gift of righteousness through faith. Teach us to trust Your promises even when we cannot see the outcome. In this season of waiting, help us rest in Your grace, walk in Your freedom, and rejoice in Your faithfulness. May our hearts be filled with hope as we await the return of Christ. In Jesus' name we pray. **Amen.**

Journal Questions

In what ways am I tempted to rely on my own efforts instead of trusting God's promises?

How can I share the hope of Christ's coming with others who feel burdened or forgotten?

What is your prayer today?

December 24

The Light of the World
Gavin King

Scripture Readings
Isaiah 9:2-7; Psalm 96; Titus 2:11-14; Luke 2:1-14, (15-20)

Focus Scripture
[2]The people walking in darkness have seen a great light; on those living in the land of deep darkness a light has dawned. [3]You have enlarged the nation and increased their joy; they rejoice before you as people rejoice at the harvest, as warriors rejoice when dividing the plunder. [6]For to us a child is born, to us a son is given, and the government will be on his shoulders. And he will be called Wonderful Counselor, Mighty God, Everlasting Father, Prince of Peace.

Isaiah 9:2-3,6 NIV

On Christmas Eve, we stand at the edge of fulfillment. The long-awaited promise is about to break into the world—not with trumpet blasts or royal fanfare, but with the cry of a newborn child. Isaiah's prophecy speaks to a weary people walking in darkness, and tonight, we remember that the light has come.

This child is no ordinary baby. He is the Wonderful Counselor, Mighty God, Everlasting Father, Prince of Peace. His birth signals the dawn of a kingdom that will never end—a reign of justice, righteousness, and peace.

In our own darkness—whether grief, fear, or uncertainty—this night reminds us that God has not forgotten us. The zeal of the Lord will accomplish His promises. The manger holds more than

55

a child; it holds hope for the world. So, we wait, not with despair, but with joy. The light has come, and He is coming again.

Prayer

Lord Jesus, we thank You for coming into our world with light and love. You are the fulfillment of every promise, the answer to every longing. Shine into our hearts today. Where there is fear, bring peace. Where there is sorrow, bring comfort. Where there is waiting, bring joy. May Your kingdom reign in us and through us, now and forever. In Jesus' name we pray. **Amen.**

Journal Questions

Where have I felt like I've been walking in darkness this year?

How has Christ's light met me in those places?

What does it mean to me personally that "a child is born" and "a son is given"?

What is your prayer today?

December 25

Good News of Great Joy
Gavin King

Scripture Readings
Isaiah 62:6-12; Psalm 97; Titus 3:4-7; Luke 2:(1-7), 8-20

Focus Scripture
[13]*Suddenly a great company of the heavenly host appeared with the angel, praising God and saying,* [14]*Glory to God in the highest heaven, and on earth peace to those on whom his favor rests.*
Luke 2:13-14 NIV

On Christmas Day, we celebrate the moment heaven touched earth. In a humble stable, the Savior of the world was born—not in splendor, but in simplicity. The angel's announcement to the shepherds wasn't reserved for kings or scholars—it was for ordinary people, reminding us that God's love reaches everyone.

This passage is filled with movement: Mary and Joseph journeying, angels proclaiming, shepherds running to see. But at its heart is stillness—a baby wrapped in cloth, lying in a manger. God's greatest gift came quietly; yet, changed everything.

The shepherds didn't just hear the good news—they responded. They went, they saw, they worshiped, and they told others. Christmas invites us to do the same: to receive the gift of Christ, rejoice in His coming, and share the wonder with the world.

Today, let your heart be filled with joy. The Savior has come. Peace is possible. Hope is alive.

Prayer

Jesus, thank You for coming near. On this day of celebration, fill our hearts with joy, our homes with peace, and our lives with Your presence. Help us respond like the shepherds—with wonder, worship, and witness. In Jesus' name we pray. **Amen.**

Journal Questions

What distractions might keep me from truly receiving the gift of Jesus?

What does it look like to "treasure and ponder" the story of Jesus, as Mary did?

How can I share the joy of Christ's birth with someone today?

What is your prayer today?

Weekly Reflection

What was the most significant spiritual moment or insight you experienced this week?

What challenges or obstacles did you encounter, and how did you overcome them?

What specific prayers have you seen answered or progress during this week?

What scripture, word, or message stood out to you and why?

In what ways can you continue to grow spiritually as you move into this next week of Advent?

Reflections

Reflections

Reflections

Reflections

www.ingramcontent.com/pod-product-compliance
Lightning Source LLC
Chambersburg PA
CBHW052214090426
42741CB00010B/2541